# MY MONSTER EATS MY VEGETABLES

WRITTEN BY

## KARLIE BURNHAM

ILLUSTRATED BY

## ANDREA STEVENSON

To my five little guys
who ALWAYS eat their
vegetables and NEVER give
them to the dog;)
-Karlie

For Fox and Sloane -the funniest,
kindest, smartest, pickiest
eaters I know.
-Andrea

He said his name was "Roger" and that he and his monster buddies had been searching for kids who didn't eat all their vegetables at dinner time.

That was me all right.
You see, at our house my mom
showed me a chart of what my
plate *should* look like for most
meals.
And fruits and vegetables...
happen to cover the BIGGEST area!
But why?
What can they even do for me?

My monster friend, Roger, helped me
understand...

At first it was AWESOME!
Roger would show up at dinner time, hide under
the table, and I would sneak him my brussels
sprouts, spinach, cooked carrots, or whatever
veggie was served that night.

A BEGINNER'S GUIDE TO

# SUPERFOODS

Roger gobbled up each one.
He even seemed to enjoy eating them.
He called them SUPERFOODS and gave
me cool facts about some of them.

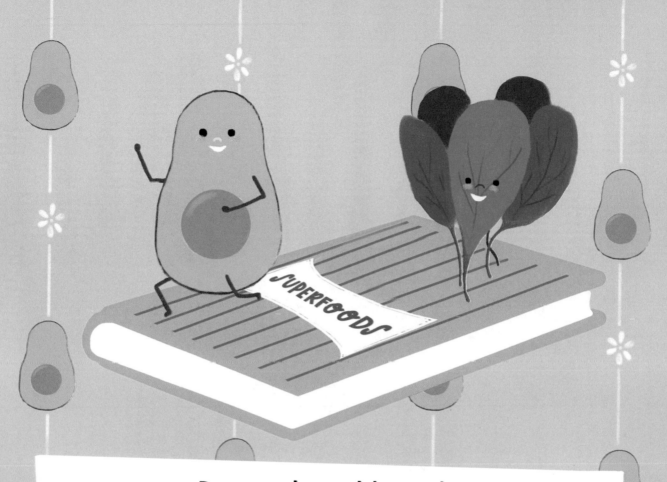

Roger also told me that
SPINACH and AVOCADOS have an
amazing amount of something called
POTASSIUM in them.
Potassium is a mineral that can help
my muscles AND my heart function properly.
WOW!

As Roger kept coming each night, and eating
more and more superfoods from my plate,
I started to notice something…

My monster friend started CHANGING.

It's true! I noticed he began looking stronger and healthier. He almost had a GLOW around him.

He would tell me of new heights he was jumping to,

new races he was running,

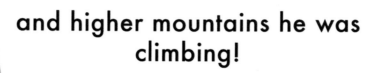
and higher mountains he was climbing!

I, on the other hand, was not feeling so great.

My energy seemed to be low, and I sure
didn't have that same glow that Roger had.

One day, I asked Roger what was making him feel so good.
"Colorful meals with vegetables, of course," he said.
"I'm lucky to have found a boy like you who gives
me so many greens each night.
My monster buddies are all jealous."

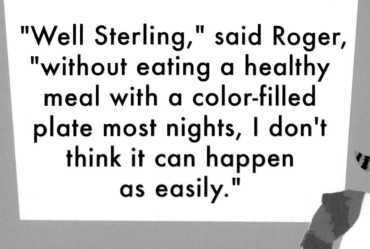

"Well Sterling," said Roger, "without eating a healthy meal with a color-filled plate most nights, I don't think it can happen as easily."

Then he left to go run another marathon.

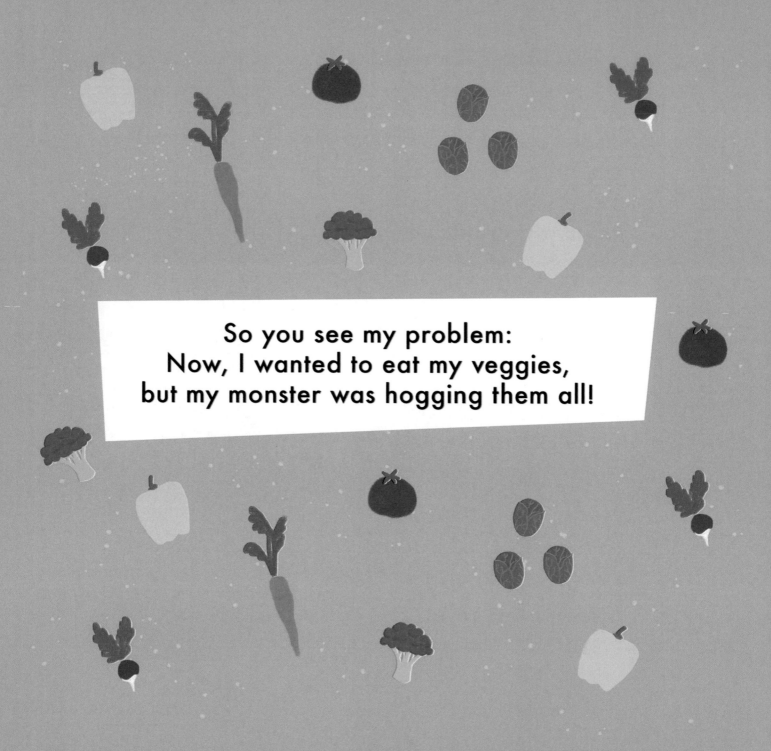

So you see my problem:
Now, I wanted to eat my veggies,
but my monster was hogging them all!

Never fear!
I came up with a
magnificent plan.

The next night I asked my mom for
a DOUBLE PORTION of broccoli.
She looked at me with a strange gleam
in her eyes, but loaded my plate.

We both happened to glance over to my brother, Curtis, at the same time. He was secretly feeding his sweet potatoes to our dog, Zorro, under the table at that EXACT moment.

Roger's eyes lit up.

# · INTRODUCING ·
# THE SUPERFOODS

## COOL CARROTS

**Serving Size:** ½ cup
**Superpower:** Carrots help keep your EYES healthy!
**How?:** Carrots are rich in something called BETA-CAROTENE which can be changed to Vitamin A in your body. Vitamin A helps keep your eyes in good health, helps protect your eyes from the rays of the sun, and lowers your chances of eye problems in the future.
**1/2 cup carrots:** 73% of your daily requirement of vitamin A

## SUPER SPINACH

**Serving Size:** 1 cup
**Superpower:** Magnesium
Spinach is rich in magnesium, which helps your body maintain muscle, nerve function, regular heart rhythm, a healthy immune system, and good blood pressure! This dark, leafy green can also help people with diabetes in several ways, including helping to lower glucose levels and increase insulin sensitivity.

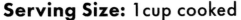

# BRILLIANT BRUSSELS SPROUTS

**Serving Size:** 1 cup cooked
**Superpower:** Antioxidant POWERHOUSE
**What are antioxidants?** They are special tools in the body that help keep your cells healthy.

One study showed that when volunteers ate about 2 cups a day, the damage at their cellular level was reduced by 30%! (health.com/nutrition).

Brussels Sprouts are also very high in fiber which means your body can go to the bathroom and get rid of waste more easily

# MIGHTY MANGOES

**Serving Size:** 1 cup sliced
**Superpower:** Potassium
**How?:** Many people think of bananas when they are looking for extra potassium, but it's MANGOES we should be seeking for potassium AND vitamin C!
**What does potassium do?** Potassium helps your heartbeat stay regular. It also helps your nerves to function and your muscles to contract!

There is close to 564 mg of potassium per mango

## SPECTACULAR SWEET POTATOES

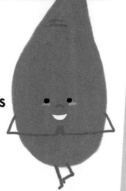

**Serving size:** One medium sweet potato
**Superpower:** Sweet and filling without spiking your blood sugar too high!
**HOW?:** Just like orange carrots, sweet potatoes have a huge amount of Vitamin A in a single serving ...in this case, more than 400% of your daily need!
They are also rich in vitamin C to boost your immune system.

## AMAZING AVOCADOS

**Serving Size:** 1 small avocado (100g)
**Superpower:** a HEALTHY fat!
**How?:** Believe it or not you need GOOD fat to help your body function properly. Your brain needs fat to help it think clearly and quickly.

Avocados are rich in this good fat. They keep you fuller longer because of that. They also have fiber in them to help satiate your appetite so you won't want to snack as much in between meals.

**Serving Size:** 1 cup
**Superpower:** Vitamin C Power!
Did you know that by eating just 1 cup of broccoli you get ALL the vitamin C your body needs for the day?? Broccoli is also higher in protein than most vegetables and still high in FIBER as well.

It is a good source of something called FOLATE, which helps your tissue growth and cell function.

What a powerhouse!!

## TERRIFIC TOMATOES

**Serving Size:** 1 small tomato
**Superpower:** Major dietary source of the antioxidant: LYCOPENE
What is lycopene? It is a nutrient that has been linked to many healthy benefits in the body including reduced risk of heart disease and cancer.

Tomatoes are also a great source of Vitamin C, potassium, folate and Vitamin K. They can be cooked and used in SO many different ways for so many different meals!

## ABOUT THE AUTHOR

Karlie Evans Burnham is an Arizona desert girl through and through. With a degree in health & wellness, Karlie loves teaching others how to eat healthier and live their best life! She stays active, thanks to 5 darling boys to whom she is blessed to be a mother to.

Follow Karlie online @Karlieburnhambooks and at KarliesCorner.com

## ABOUT THE ILLUSTRATOR

Andrea Stevenson is an artist, designer, and illustrator from the hot, hot desert of Arizona. When not doodling or snacking on breakfast foods, she busies herself by reading, imagining with her two children, and watching movies with happy endings.

Made in the USA
Middletown, DE
12 March 2022